WORLD PRAYERS, MANTRAS, & WORDS OF POWER

ANCIENT AND CONTEMPORARY WISDOM FOR A NEW AGE

D1722733

ALIX H. MAHÉ

ISBN: 1-4392-6800-2
ISBN-13: 9781439268001

Prayer is the medium of Miracles

"A Course in Miracles"

TABLE OF CONTENTS

PREFACE

This book is the result of my own quest for a compilation of simple prayers expressing no particular dogmatic attachment but reflecting my interest and curiosity in all religions and cultures of this world. At a time of what were for me personal life changes and intense soul searching, the image of this collection came to me in a dream.

A mantra, the sound of the primordial universe and creator, is said to release its power and bring enlightenment when chanted in its specific tempo. Sutras help us bring enlightenment to earth, whereas incantations might ask for protection or peace. They remind us of the place of the sacred in our life. All are powerful, to be respected and never underestimated.

Prayers for peace are universal and are sung out in one voice, offered by every human tradition. Light has also always been the privileged representation of ascended masters and the Godhead itself. Some incantations have been channeled to humanity, in preparation of a New Age.

This compilation is an introduction to, and your possible first encounter with, many other cultures, religions, and movements. To some of you, a page will reflect familiar and cherished grounds. To others, the words will engender curiosity and a desire to learn more. The commentaries are mine only, presented to you as a simple and basic explanation of the context of the text origins.

This book is meant as a gift, without ties or hidden agendas. Take what you will from it, what feels true and of value to you. All of it is a blessing.

ACKNOWLEDGEMENTS

First and foremost, I would like to thank my mentor and teacher, Amy Thakurdas.

Friend, healer, hula sister, and spiritual adviser, Amy has been a most influential figure in my life for many years. Even though this book is a personal endeavor, it would not have come to be without her wise suggestions, endless support, caring affection, and all those kicks in my derrière!

Gratitude is extended to all of you who have contributed to making this possible, one way or another. Over this lifetime, I have read more books than can be counted. Even though it is an impossible task to list them all, I am deeply appreciative of the knowledge and tools they have given me.

I heard many times: "You should write a book," reinforcing a lifelong feeling that the printed work would be my preferred medium of creativity. Those of you who have listened to my "lectures," talks, and advise on many subjects and allowed me to introduce or explain new things, I thank as well. I became the teacher and guide that I enjoy being when you did not ask me to stop. I hope that I will continue to open doors for you.

Thank you to my daughters, who put their fears aside during that summer when I quit my job to write this book, so that I could do this for me. Merci also to all the friends whose encouragement and feedback led to this publication.

My thanks also go to my publishing team, who has helped make this crazy dream come to be.

Introduction

Prayers, mantras, incantations. Humanity has voiced them as long as there has been the notion of a Higher Power. Whether prayers of supplication, requests for guidance or intercession, expressions of thankfulness, praises of the Almighty, silent meditative contemplations, or appeals for a blessing, healing or protection, they are the privileged way of communication and union with the Divine. A mystical dialogue both inner and outward and the study of the meaning of life and subsequent enlightenment, this experience can be life-changing in its revelations or humbling in its self-examination.

You will find many examples of prayers here. Some may be unknown or even quite different than what you hold a prayer to be. They have Light and Peace in common, though, representing the Godhead and His/Her representation on this earth. These texts are not inclusively representative of their origin, but universal in their meaning and message. Light has been the preferred way of receiving grace and blessings for humanity, and it is what keeps me inspired on my hopeful way to enlightenment.

This gathering of prayers, dear reader, is meant for you to be appreciated as per your need or inspiration. Many movements, cultures, and places of the earth are represented here. I have not meant for any to be privileged, preferred, or chosen over another. On the contrary, I am convinced that the universality of the meaning overwhelms the possible unease felt at the reading or uttering of someone else's holy words. You can change a divine name, yet the message remains unchanged. Whether you pray to God, Christ, Allah, Yahweh, All That Is, Spirit, or another entity, I believe the purity of the soul and the conviction of the heart transcend any specific provenance or identity.

I trust that you, dear reader, will feel inspired, uplifted, helped, and connected to the Divine Light while reading these words. The images will be, I hope, a source of beauty and inspiration to you as well.

The information published has been collected to reflect beliefs of tradition, culture, and religion as clearly as I understand them. I do not presume to call myself an expert, nor do I wish to simplify any message or philosophy presented here. The impossible task of presenting a subject so vast and complex with a few words should not be interpreted as a reflection of its importance. The individual is asked to ponder meaning, message, and value, using her/his free will. I merely offer you the opportunity to discover something new, maybe tease your curiosity into wanting to learn more. I apologize for any offense I may cause; my intent has never been to misrepresent or alter any of these. Complete respect and deep gratitude is offered to all. As for any omission or oversight of a specific religion or philosophy, it is unintentional.

All I humbly ask for is a curious mind, an open heart, and a receptive soul. The time is upon us when all will realize that all is One.

PART I

WORLD PRAYERS, MANTRAS, AND WORDS OF POWER

The Peace Prayer

St. Francis of Assisi

Lord, make me an instrument of Thy peace
Where there is hatred, let me sow love;
Where there is injury, pardon;
Where there is error, the truth;
Where there is doubt, the faith;
Where there is despair, hope;
Where there is darkness, light;
And where there is sadness, joy.

O Divine Master,
Grant that I may not so much seek
To be consoled, as to console;
To be understood, as to understand;
To be loved, as to love.
For it is in giving that we receive;
It is in pardoning that we are pardoned;
And it is in dying that we are born to eternal life.
Amen.

Gâyatrî Mantra

Hinduism

Aum
Bhuh Bhuvah Svah
Tat Savitur Varenyam
Bhargo Devasya Dheemahi
Dhiyo Yo nah Prachodayat

Om
We meditate on the radiance of that Supreme Divine Being,
The Creator of the world planes,
Earth, heaven and those spaces in between
May that Divine Being direct our intelligence

Translation by Swami Adiswarananda

Prayer for Peace

Hazrat Inayat Khan

Send Thy peace O Lord, which is
perfect and everlasting,
that our souls may radiate peace.

Send Thy peace O Lord, that we
may think, act, and speak harmoniously.

Send Thy peace O Lord, that we
may be contented and thankful for
Thy bountiful gifts.

Send Thy peace O Lord, that amidst
our worldly strife, we may enjoy Thy bliss.

Send Thy peace O Lord, that we
may endure all, tolerate all, in the thought of
Thy grace and mercy.

Send Thy peace O Lord, that our lives
may become a Divine vision and in Thy light,
all darkness may vanish.

Send Thy peace O Lord, our Father and Mother,
that we Thy children on Earth may all
unite in one family.

"O Great Spirit"

Lakota Chief Yellow Lark

Oh, Great Spirit,
whose voice I hear in the winds
and whose breath gives life to all the world, hear me.
I am small and weak.
I need your strength and wisdom.

Let me walk in beauty and make my eyes
ever behold the red and purple sunset.
Make my hands respect the things you have made
and my ears sharp to hear your voice.
Make me wise so that I may understand
the things you have taught my people.
Let me learn the lessons you have hidden
in every leaf and rock.

I seek strength, not to be superior to my brother,
but to fight my greatest enemy—myself.
Make me always ready to come to you
with clean hands and straight eyes,
so when life fades, as the fading sunset,
my spirit will come to you
without shame.

GUIDANCE PRAYER

JUDAISM

DEAR LORD,

CLOSE MY EYES FROM EVIL,

AND MY EARS FROM HEARING IDLE WORDS,

AND MY HEART FROM REFLECTING UNCHASTE THOUGHTS,

AND MY VEINS FROM THINKING OF TRANSGRESSIONS.

GUIDE MY FEET TO WALK IN THY COMMANDMENTS

AND THY RIGHTEOUS WAYS,

AND MAY THY MERCIES BE TURNED UPON ME.

Mantra of Compassion

Buddhism

I invoke the transformation and purification of the six negative emotions of pride, jealousy, desire, ignorance, greed and anger into their true nature, enlightened mind.

Spiritual Eye Prayer

Yogananda

Heavenly Father,
Open my spiritual eye
so that I can enter Thy kingdom of
omnipresence.
Father,
do not leave me behind in this mortal
world of misery

Lead me from darkness to light
From death to immortality
From ignorance to endless wisdom
From sorrow to eternal joy.

"We Return Thanks"

Iroquois

We return thanks to our mother,
the earth, which sustains us.
We return thanks to the rivers and streams,
which supply us with water.
We return thanks to all herbs, which furnish
medicines
for the cure of our diseases.
We return thanks to the corn, and to her sisters,
the beans and squashes, which give us life.
We return thanks to the bushes and trees,
which provide us with fruit.
We return thanks to the wind,
which, moving the air, has banished diseases.
We return thanks to the moon and the stars,
which have given us their light when the sun
was gone.
We return thanks to our grandfather He-no,
that he has protected his grandchildren
from witches and reptiles, and has given us his rain.
We return thanks to the sun,
that he has looked upon the earth with a
beneficent eye.
Lastly, we return thanks to the Great Spirit,
in whom is embodied all goodness,
and who directs all things for the good of his
children.

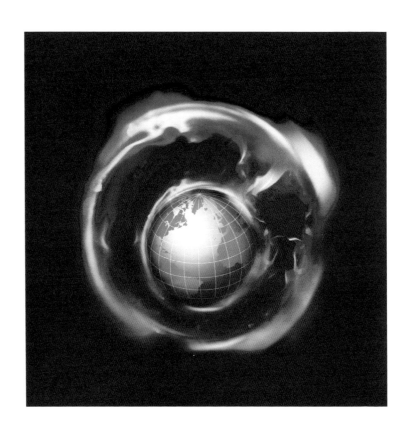

The Healing Prayer

Hazrat Inayat Khan

Beloved Lord, Almighty God,
Through the Rays of the Sun,
Through the Waves of the Air,
Through the All Pervading Life in Space;
Purify and Revivify Us
And we pray, heal our bodies, hearts, and souls.
Amen

The Serenity Prayer

Reinhold Niebuhr

God, give us grace to accept with serenity
the things that cannot be changed,
courage to change the things
which should be changed,
and the wisdom to distinguish
the one from the other.

Living one day at a time,
enjoying one moment at a time,
accepting hardship as a pathway to peace,
taking, as Jesus did,
this sinful world as it is,
not as I would have it,
trusting that You will make all things right,
if I surrender to Your will,
so that I may be reasonably happy in this life,
and supremely happy with You forever in the next.

Amen.

The Great Invocation

Maitreya

From the point of Light within the Mind of God
Let light stream forth into the minds of men.
Let Light descend on Earth.

From the point of Love within the Heart of God
Let love stream forth into the hearts of men.
May Christ return to Earth.

From the centre where the Will of God is known
Let purpose guide the little wills of men—
The Purpose which the Masters know and serve.

From the centre which we call the race of men
Let the Plan of Love and Light work out.
And may it seal the door where evil dwells.

Let Light and Love and Power restore the Plan
on Earth.

OM

OM MANI PADME HUM

Tibetan pronounciation—Om Mani Pémé Hung

Prayer to Practice the Golden Rule

Eusebius of Caesarea

Dear Lord,
May I be no man's enemy,
   and may I be the friend of that which is eternal
   and abides.

May I never quarrel with those nearest me;
   and if I do, may I be reconciled quickly.

May I never devise evil against any person.
   If any devise evil against me, may I escape
   uninjured and without the need of hurting them.

May I love, seek, and attain only that which is good.
   May I wish for all humanity's happiness and envy
   none.

May I, to the extent of my power,
   give all needful help to my friends and to all who
   are in want.

May I respect myself.
   May I always keep tame that which rages in me.

May I accustom myself to be gentle,
   and never be angry with people because of
   circumstances.

May I never discuss who is wicked
   and what wicked things he has done,
   but know good people and follow in their footsteps

Light Invocation

DaEl Walker

I invoke the Light of God within
I am a clear and perfect channel of Light and Love
Light is my guide

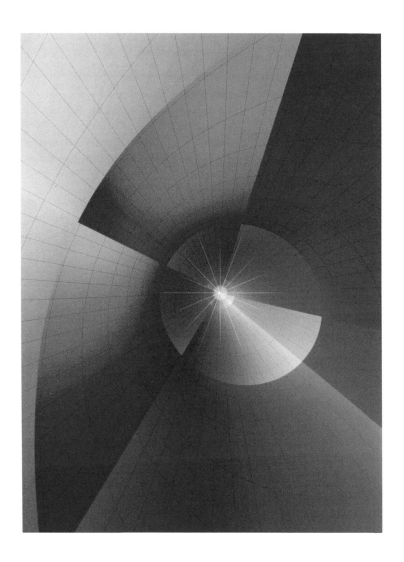

Presence of the Divine Light

Sri Swami Satchidananda

O Lord, the Light of Lights,
You are the Indweller of the entire Universe.
You are the One who makes the sun shine, the moon shine,
who makes the stars shine, who makes the fire burn.
Kindly lead us to that Light of Wisdom
and remove the darkness of ignorance; enlighten our hearts.

Help us experience that Light within and without.
Help us see the same Light, the same spirit dwelling everywhere
in everything, or, to be more accurate, as everything.
Let us behold Your spirit running through all.
Give us the strength and courage and capacity to experience
that peace and joy within and share the same with everyone.

Help us to get away from these selfish temptations with which
we are creating all the differences, all the fights, and all the wars.
Please guide us to know our brothers and sisters
and to know we are all parts of Your family.
Enlighten our paths, O Light of Lights, Lord of Lords.
Help us, guide us.

PRAYER FOR PEACE

ZOROASTRIANISM

WE PRAY TO GOD

TO ERADICATE ALL THE MISERY IN THE WORLD:

THAT UNDERSTANDING TRIUMPH OVER
IGNORANCE,

THAT GENEROSITY TRIUMPH OVER INDIFFERENCE,

THAT TRUST TRIUMPH OVER CONTEMPT, AND

THAT TRUTH TRIUMPH OVER FALSEHOOD.

"Disturb Us, Lord"

Sir Francis Drake

Disturb us, Lord, when
We are too well pleased with ourselves,
When our dreams have come true
Because we have dreamed too little,
When we arrived safely
Because we sailed too close to the shore.

Disturb us, Lord, when
With the abundance of things we possess
We have lost our thirst
For the waters of life;
Having fallen in love with life,
We have ceased to dream of eternity
And in our efforts to build a new earth,
We have allowed our vision
Of the new Heaven to dim.

Disturb us, Lord, to dare more boldly,
To venture on wider seas
Where storms will show your mastery;
Where losing sight of land,
We shall find the stars.
We ask You to push back
The horizons of our hopes;
And to push into the future
In strength, courage, hope, and love.

Lotus Sutra

Nichiren Buddhism

Nam Myoho Renge Kyo

Fire Blessing

Aborigine

May the fire be in our thoughts
Making them true, good and just
May it protect us from the evil one.

May the fire be in our eyes;
May it open our eyes to share what is good in life.
We ask that the fire may protect us
From what is not rightfully ours.

We ask that the fire be on our lips
So that we may speak the truth in kindness;
That we may serve, and encourage others.
May it protect us from speaking evil.

May the fire be in our ears.
We pray that we may hear with a deep,
deep listening;
So that we may hear the flow of water,
And of all Creation, and the Dreaming.
May we be protected from gossip and from things
That harm and break down our family.

May the fire be in our arms and hands
So that we may be of service and build up love.
May the fire protect us from all violence.

May the fire be in our whole being, in
our legs and feet,
Enable us to walk the earth with reverence and care
So that we may walk in the ways of goodness
and truth
And be protected from walking away from
what is truth.

Prosperity Prayer

Zen Buddhism

May all beings in the three evil paths of existence
variously suffering the eight kinds of disasters
be thereby released from the afflictions!
May all beings in the triple world who are recipients
of the fourfold benefaction thereby participate in the
merit!

May the state continue in peaceful prosperity
with all its warlike activities stopped!
May the wind blow in time, the rain fall seasonably,
and the people live happily!
May the entire congregation sharing in the exercise
cherish the higher aspirations!
To go beyond the ten stages with a cap, and this without
much difficulty!

May this congregation keep on its quiet life, free from
disturbances.
And the patrons and devotees grow not only in faith
but in wisdom and bliss!
We pray this to all the Buddhas and Bodhisattva-
Mahasattvas
in the ten quarters, of the past, present, and future,
and to Mahaprajna-paramita!

Peace Prayer

Kikuyu

Praise ye Lord,
Peace be with us.

Say that the elders may have wisdom and speak with
one voice.
Peace be with us.

Say that the country may have tranquility.
Peace be with us.

And the people may continue to increase.
Peace be with us.

Say that the people and the flock and the herds
May prosper and be free from illness.
Peace be with us.

Say that the fields may bear much fruit
And the land may continue to be fertile.
Peace be with us.

May peace reign over earth,
May the gourd cup agree with vessel.
Peace be with us.

May their heads agree and every ill word be driven out
Into the wilderness, into the virgin forest.

Muhammad's Prayer

Islam

O God,
give me light in my heart
and light in my tongue
and light in my hearing
and light in my sight
and light in my feeling
and light in all body
and light before me
and light behind me.

Give me, I pray Thee,
Light on my right hand
And light on my left hand
And light above me
And light beneath me,

O Lord,
Increase light within me
And give me light
And illuminate me.

Spirit Prayer

'Abdu'l-baha

O God!
Refresh and gladden my spirit.
Purify my heart, illuminate my powers.
I lay all of my affairs in Thy hand.
Thou art my guide and my refuge.
I will no longer be sorrowful and grieved;
I will be a happy and joyful being.
O God!
I will no longer be full of anxiety,
Nor will I let trouble harass me.
I will not dwell on the unpleasant things
of life.
O God!
Thou art more friend to me than I am to
myself
I dedicate myself to Thee, O Lord.

Protection Prayer

Isabel Hickey

I clothe myself with a Robe of Light,
composed of the Love, Wisdom, and Power
of God.
Not only for my own protection,
but for all who see it and come in contact
with it
will be drawn to God and healed.

PART II

COMMENTARIES AND NOTES

THE PEACE PRAYER/
ST. FRANCIS OF ASSISI

St. Francis of Assisi

Born in thirteenth century Italy, St. Francis, a soldier, lived a privileged existence. The divine revelation, "Follow the Master not the man," led to his embracing poverty and becoming a traveling hermit, spreading the Gospel all the way to the Middle East. Repairing churches and leading a penitent life, he preached spirituality rooted in the Gospels.

His ability to speak to animals and birds has given him the title of Saint of Ecology. He founded the order of the Franciscans and the feminine order of the Poor Clares.

Christianity

Following the Jewish tradition, Christianity is seen as the new covenant with God through the Messiah ("anointed") Jesus Christ. God's message is given through the Gospel (or New Testament of the Bible) as preached by Jesus and compiled by disciples. Jesus Christ is thought of as the embodiment of God on earth.

The Almighty is seen through the Trinity: Father (creator), Son (savior) and the Holy Spirit (inspiration, unifying force). Sin is at the basis of the loss of humankind's harmonious and perfect connection to God. Salvation depends on outside and divine assistance, the Grace that gives triumph over one's low or evil nature. Individual will and deeds can transform one's nature with the help of Grace within us.

Man's sins, the thoughts or actions that betray the moral principles set in the Ten Commandments and by the Gospel, prevent his return to Paradise after death. The expulsion of Adam and Eve from the Garden of Eden has resulted in countless generations enduring suffering, disease, and pain. Hell (where the devil dwells and suffering is infinite), or purgatory (the holding place where sins must be expiated before entering paradise), can, however, be avoided by leading a life that follows the Gospel. Divine judgment at the time of death will determine one's place in the afterlife.

Man's redemption from sin depends on repentance and the acceptance of salvation through Jesus Christ. Belief in unalterable truths, such as the perfection of God and his creation, the power of forgiveness, the acceptance that Jesus Christ died as redemption to the sins of humanity, stands at the foundation of the faith.

The faith holds the Bible, comprised of the Old Testament (shared with the Jewish and Muslim faiths) and the New Testament (compilation of the life and teachings of Jesus), as the sacred book containing the God's truth. Literal readings versus respectful guidance have divided the faith for centuries.

Rites such as baptism (the immersion in or sprinkling of holy water to signify one's entry into the fold), communion, daily prayer, the Eucharist (receiving of symbolic wine and bread representing the last meals of Jesus and his twelve Apostles) at church on Sunday services, confession (admission of sins), and penance (punishment) are keys to salvation for many Christians, especially Catholics. Evangelical Christians may follow the spontaneous guidance and influence of the Holy Spirit rather than perform exact rites. They may use tools as different as contemporary music, faith healing, mass media or the charismatic personality of a minister, during worship and to spread the Gospel.

The passage of two millennia, disagreement on credo, ethnic, and cultural differences, the varying sway of political authorities, philosophical ideas, the influence of saints (a holy person who has reached Paradise) or monastic figures, and the integration of older pagan religions have divided Christianity into countless churches, including Catholicism, Coptic, Protestantism, Mormonism, and Greek Orthodoxy. While the belief in Jesus Christ remains unchanged, rituals, expression, and celebration of the faith vary enormously.

Catholics honor the Pope as the present Apostle of Jesus and the Head of the Church, worship Mother Mary, call upon the saints, and believe in a purgatory as well as in inner grace. The all-male clergy keeps vows of chastity, and follows strict guidance in worship and credo. Protestantism was raised with Martin Luther in fifteenth century Germany as a reaction to the perceived corruption of Catholicism, demanding the return to the traditional interpretation of the Scriptures. Luther's translation in German of the Bible and the publication of his theses ultimately led to the schism with the church. Guttenberg's invention of the printing press allowed the mass distribution of religious texts, up to then written in Latin and only accessible to the priestly hierarchy, and accelerated the spread of Protestant ideas. Ministers and pastors marry and are not considered separate from the ordinary believer.

Renditions of the faith in architecture, paintings, music, literature, and other artistic forms tell the story of its strength and depth through time.

Major celebrations recall the life of Christ and include Christmas on December twenty-fifth (celebration of his birth) and Easter in the springtime (recalling his Last Supper, crucifixion, then resurrection).

Jesus Christ

Jesus was a man who was filled with the presence of God, a human being through whom the will and the words of God are revealed.

Born Jewish of the Virgin Mary near Jerusalem (in present Israel) under signs of his Messianic arrival, he was sin-free. Baptized at age thirty, his life turned to prophesying and spreading the Gospel. He preached the love of God and of one's fellow human beings, entering into a new covenant.

The miracles he performed, his incendiary political and dogmatic teachings for his time, and a growing number of followers brought him in conflict with the Jewish High Priest and the Roman governor of Palestine. He was condemned to death by crucifixion in Jerusalem. Resurrected three days later before ascending to heaven, his death and subsequent resurrection are powerful messages. Redemption and salvation restore the privileged connection to God, offer entrance to paradise after death, and guarantee a positive outcome on the last judgment day.

Christians worship Jesus Christ as the Savior of humanity and the redeemer of all sin. Muslims see him as one of the great Prophets of Islam. Jews do not acknowledge him as their Messiah. Certain New Age movements see Jesus as a separate man, overshadowed during the last three years of his life by the Ascended Master Christ.

GÂYATRÎ MANTRA / HINDUISM

Gâyatrî Mantra

The mantra originates in the Rig Veda and is considered the most important of all mantras. It starts and ends with OM, the most sacred word and sound, embodying every sacred mantra. The Hindu tradition praises it as containing wisdom and enlightenment.

Hinduism

Hinduism, the world's third largest religion, represents a broad range of religious concepts, sharing ideas, beliefs, and customs that have been evolving throughout centuries. It did not start with a specific founder or event, nor does it offer a specific credo or organized rites. It traces its origin to India, with many other geographical and philosophical influences.

Man learns to live in the world but does not renounce it. Detachment from material things, practicing the right way of living, and devotion to God lead to self-realization. The mastering and control of the senses, thoughts, and feelings is obtained through the practice of yoga.

Though Hinduism holds a complex pantheon of deities with their own followers, temples, colorful feasts, and rituals, all are usually believed to be forms of a single powerful being/Spirit, Brahman, whose different aspects are manifested in separate incarnations.

Foundations of Hinduism are: Samsara, Mokhsha, Karma, Dharma, and Ahimsa. Samsara, the ongoing cycle of reincarnation of the soul (called Atman) follows the law of Karma. Rebirth of a soul into an earth form must continue as it follows the path towards Moksha (the end of the cycle) and its reunification with Brahman, the Ultimate Truth.

As the cosmic law by which the consequences of one's actions will be felt into future lives, Karma determines one's circumstances. Good Karma obtained in a lifetime will ensure a better circumstance next time.

Dharma encompasses obligatory rituals as well as one's duties to the family and social group. This code of ethics is embodied in the practice of yoga, meaning union, the privileged way and practice to reach Moksha.

Ahimsa, the principle of nonviolence, expresses the belief that killing and eating animal flesh is detrimental to one's path toward Moksha. Hindus are vegetarians, all animal life being considered sacred and the present incarnation of a soul.

These principles are also essential pillars of Jainism and Buddhism.

Unlike other religions, Hinduism's divine revelations were directly given into the books of knowledge, named Vedas, and handed down orally by Brahmins, or priests, through generations, and eventually written down.

The Vedas are the embodiment of truth, and lead seekers to eternal bliss and Moksha through rites and incantations. Divinely revealed, they contain four sacred books: Rig-Veda, Yajur-Veda, Sama-Veda and Athaarva-Veda, which in turn contain four parts. Their origin probably traces back 3,500 years.

Important writings of Vedic philosophy were compiled centuries later and include the Upanishads, which further explain the basic concepts relating to the nature of man and his self-realization.

The Puranas describe the origin of the cosmology and the history of gods and heroes, fostering the development of a myriad of deity cults. It describes the rise of the great deities (Brahma the creator, Vishnu the preserver, Shiva the destroyer), who constitute Hinduism's Trinity or Trimurti. Feminine energies are seen embodied by the goddesses Devi, Lakshmi, Parvati, and Kali, among many others.

The Mahabharata and Ramayana, long epic poems of divine inspiration, were written centuries after the Vedas. They offer stories of a moral substance. The Bhagavat Gita, part of the Mahabharata, sits at the heart of the Hindu faith. A dialog between the god Krishna and the warrior Arjuna, it contains myths and legends, philosophical reflections, discussions on ethics, moral guidance, and meditations. It expresses the Hindu spiritual philosophy and teachings in an accessible way.

At a local level, the local ruler not only had temporal power, but he was also the divine's representation and his mediator, merging religion into everyday life. The controversial caste system still prevalent in parts of India is not Hindu in origin, though it resembles the system of Varna, which categorized society in 4 social classes. Relying on the principle of Karma and Brahmins being the highest group, the caste structure has socio-economic, political and ethnic sources.

The stories and legends of kings, demons, and avatars (incarnations) of the deities (i.e., Krishna as the eighth incarnation of Vishnu) have led to artistic renditions in every medium. Timeless traditions include recitations of the sacred texts, sacred dances, sculptures and paintings in a thousand colors. Temples are the cornerstone of Hindu life, consecrated to numerous deities and holding specific ceremonies throughout the day and year. Festivals are as alive today as they were centuries ago.

Many aspects of Hinduism are now global, bare of their strictly religious nature. The practice of yoga, meditation, and ahimsa has spread around the world. Karma has become part of our everyday vocabulary.

Prayer for Peace
The Healing Prayer/
Hazrat Inayat Khan

Hazrat Inayat Khan

Hazrat Inayat Khan was born a Sufi Muslim in India in 1882. His family was well known for its contribution to music. He was exposed to many visiting philosophers, musicians, and religious figures while being brought up in a household that encouraged tolerance and spiritual development.

He studied with Sufi teachers throughout the subcontinent for years, feeling that chanting and music were spiritual links to God. Touring India as a celebrated musician, he met the Sufi Master who helped guide him on his spiritual path, and told him to unite the West and the East with the magic of music.

Traveling through America and Europe in the 1910s and 1920s, he taught Sufism and the oneness of all religions. He founded the Sufi Order in the West and set residence near Paris, France.

The rituals and practices he established tell of his belief in the universality of spiritualism. All major religions and holy words are drawn upon for enlightenment, and individuals of many origins are honored for their contributions to humanity. His followers are left free to worship at temples of their choice and follow a chosen religion, harmonious to his teachings.

His peaceful message aims at world unity, transcending all differences, and fulfilling one's religion through one's way of life.

Sufism

Beginning a century later than Islam, Sufism represents its mystical side, the search for spiritual awareness through a simple, almost ascetic life inspired by Sufi writers and poets such as Rumi.

While Muslims believe closeness to God comes after death, Sufis aim to experience it during their lifetime. Furthermore, it is one's highest purpose. Love is the means to reconnect to the divine source of all existence. The spiritual progress of the adept comes through disciplined stages and strict practices, which can only be revealed by a master.

While following traditional Islamic laws, Sufism achieves inner enlightenment through detachment from the material, nonviolence, and control over one's negative tendencies or ego (Nafs). Fasting, contemplation, meditation, and Dhikr, the recitation and invocation of God's names, are essential practices.

Listening to and playing music as a tool to reach higher stages of awareness has been controversial with

Muslims, whose teachings do not accept this practice. Sufis believe that music represents the expression of the perfect harmony of the universe and its laws, the picture of God freed of form or thought. It is thought to bring great spiritual blessings.

Twirling Sufi dervishes, dancing while in a trance, repeat the name of God, attaining a state where only God's presence is felt. Others in India, called fakirs, are said to possess magical and advanced powers, obtained through specific methods of progression on their spiritual journey. They are ascetics, who choose to renounce the physical world.

Because Sufism is the essence at the heart of every religion, it is in harmony with all. Its message of religious tolerance, universal harmony, respect for all and divine love attract Muslims as well as non-Muslims of all creeds.

Please refer to the "Islam" section under "Muhammad's Prayer/Islam"

"O Great Spirit" / Lakota

Lakota

Chief Yellow Lark translated this prayer of the Lakota Nation in 1887.

A part of the Sioux nation, the Lakotas, whose name means "alliance of friends," follow the Native American belief that everything and everyone belong to the cycle of life. All stand equal as divine.

"Great Spirit" or "Great Mystery" is not a god in a human form, but is the universal force that creates all. Every person, plant, animal, rock, and place has a spirit, and their healthy union guarantees the thriving and survival of all. Each part of this whole is worshipped and thanked, understood to be indispensable and worthy of respect. Animals hold a special place as spiritual companions and the symbol of a preferred quality of character. A simple walk reminds the individual of his/her place in the order of things, of the blessings that are given, and of the need to maintain this state of interdependence.

The necessity to live in harmony with nature in order to maintain balance and order in the larger universe is taught as a way of life, not as religious dogma. The absence of organized structure, priests, or temples is replaced by strict rules and expectations for a decent and ethically responsible life. While faith is experienced in a private manner, peace and harmony must be reached and maintained within oneself first, then with other members of the community, as well as with nature and the universe.

In this context, personal responsibility in everyday deeds is of utmost importance. Meditation and silent retreats are useful tools. Considered part of the life cycle, the ancestors retain a valuable place, and reincarnation is an accepted belief.

Rituals such as the seven sacred ceremonies prepare girls for adulthood, ask for visions and guidance, honor and strengthen relationships, and attend to the souls of the departed. They teach values, beliefs, and sacred traditions. Including dancing, drumming, sacred pipe smoking, purifying one's body and soul, and feasting, they are observed at specific time of year and moon cycles. Nature plays a significant place in those rituals.

These were a gift to the Lakotas by "White Buffalo Calf Woman," a sacred messenger. They are: the "keeping of the soul" (funeral rite), the "Rite of Purification" (cleansing ceremony for the soul), the "Vision Quest" (reaching a higher awareness), the "Sun Dance" (communal ceremony of fasting and dancing in order to help those who need spiritual assistance), the "Making of Relatives" (sharing of gifts and oneself to strengthen relationships), the "Puberty Rite" (honoring pubescent girls as women), and the "Throwing of the Ball" (elaborate ball game).

Special members of the tribe known as shamans serve as intermediaries with the spirit world for healing, spiritual renewal, and the good of the community. They maintain or restore the harmony between dimensions. They can diagnose an illness, restore health and balance using their healing powers, herbs, or rocks, and receive guidance through trances or visions.

GUIDANCE PRAYER / JUDAISM

Judaism

The oldest of the three monotheist faiths and native of Palestine, Judaism traces its credo from the Tanach (Bible), which contains the five books of the Old Testament, also called Torah. Jews believe that the present covenant with God through Moses is still in effect, until an anointed king (Messiah) declares himself and brings God's kingdom to earth.

The Torah tells the story of the creation and of the children of Israel, the fall of humanity, the flood, and of the covenants between God and humanity through divinely inspired individuals. Among those, Abraham is the father figure and founder, who sealed the original covenant with Yahweh; Moses who led the Hebrews from Egypt to the Promised Land received the Ten Commandments from God; Noah built the ark that saved his family and two of each animals from the forty-day flood; and Jacob, who dreamed of a ladder to heaven, is the father of the twelve tribes of Israel.

The Tanach also contains guidance laws, such as the dietary Kosher law, and the Ten Commandments given to Moses, also at the basis of Christianity. These are: (1) You shall have no other gods before me; (2) You shall not make for yourself a carved image—any likeness of anything that is in heaven above, or that is in the earth beneath, or that is in the water under the earth; (3) You shall not take the name of the Lord your God in vain; (4) Remember the Sabbath day, to keep it holy; (5) Honor your father and your mother; (6) You shall not murder; (7) You shall not commit adultery; (8) You shall not steal; (9) You shall not bear false witness against your neighbor; (10) You shall not covet your neighbor's house, your neighbor's wife, nor his male servant, nor his female servant, nor his ox, nor his donkey, nor anything that is your neighbor's.

Following the Diaspora ("scattering" of the Jewish people after the defeats against Rome in the first century), two major schools of thought emerged, the Sephardim in Northern Africa and the Middle East, and the Ashkenazim in Europe.

Judaism was first rebuilt around the Mishna, Jewish laws also known as Oral Law organized and codified by Rabbi Judah in the third century. Rabbis throughout the next centuries and of various geographical locations further interpreted the Mishna. Their interpretations and commentaries were recorded in the books of Talmud and Gemara. Applying the traditional laws to their present circumstances, the guidelines given in the Holy Books are incorporated in everyday life.

Traditional celebrations recall Israel's history and rites of passage remain essential in the practice of Judaism today. A bar/bat mitzvah celebrates a teenager's coming of age. The four major celebrations are Pessach (or Passover, recalling the Hebrews' exodus from Egypt), Rosh Hashana (the new year celebrated in the fall), Yom Kippur (Day of Atonement eight days after the New Year) and Hanukkah (commemorating the miracle of the lights, which lasts eight days in the winter time). Prayers are chanted in Hebrew, as the reading and studying of the Holy Books is done.

The creation of the state of Israel in 1948 was sparked by the Zionist movement, which had been calling for a Jewish homeland without waiting for the emergence of the Messiah. A quest for survival following centuries of widespread anti-Semitism and the holocaust of six million Jews in Nazi Germany and the need to return to the ancestral home to prepare for the Messiah's arrival added to the political decision. Israel's existence has led to several wars and continued conflict with her Arab neighbors.

Though observance of the laws vary among groups and individuals, the idea of God having chosen the Jewish people to hold his covenant with humanity remains the cornerstone of the faith.

It is interesting to note that Abraham gave birth to the Jewish people through his son Isaac, and to the Arabic people through his son Ishmael. Islam recognizes Abraham, Noah and Moses as prophets, as does Christianity.

Mantra of Compassion Om/Buddhism

Buddhism

Siddhartha Gautama founded Buddhism, the fourth largest world religion, about 2,500 years ago in Northern India. Followers do not worship him as a God, but as the man who found the answer of Dharma (truth) inside himself and achieved Enlightenment (Buddha). He is the path, not the goal.

Buddhism explains the state of the world and the unhappiness of people by the Four Noble Truths: (1) Life is suffering; (2) Suffering is caused by attachment, whether it be to people, things, or ideas; (3) Living in the present and giving up attachments leads to happiness; (4) Following the eight-fold path points the way to the inner state of Nirvana, or freedom from suffering.

The eight-fold path (right understanding, right thoughts, right speech, right action, right livelihood, right effort, right mindfulness, and right concentration) guides man to happiness and toward the release of the reincarnation cycle.

One finds enlightenment outside of an ascetic path or external entity by following the "middle way" and a moral code of conduct. Constant mindfulness of one's thoughts and behavior is at the core of the teaching, with compassion at the heart of its wisdom. One is responsible for one's karma and therefore destiny, but also for others who are affected by his deeds. The qualities of openness, sympathy, caring, tolerance, generosity, patience are cultivated. In understanding one's impact on others and the world, does one gain true knowledge and wisdom, which create inner change.

In this teaching of tolerance, mindfulness, non-violence and the necessity of inner work, Buddhism ties with Hinduism and Jainism. Many, who cite its lack of strict dogma, priestly hierarchy and imposed rites as the reason why it is not truly a religion, call Buddhism a philosophy.

Several schools of thought emerged with the spread of Buddhism in Asia. Zen is mostly found in Japan, Theravada is prevalent today in South East Asia and the Indian subcontinent, but the ancient Mahayana tradition of Bodhisattvas remains strong.

These enlightened beings chose to renounce Nirvana, and the end of their karmic/reincarnation cycle in order to return to earth out of compassion. They can intervene in human lives and lead them to salvation. Often represented in mandalas, they are called upon by followers, asking for help and guidance. Circular symbolic representations of the cosmos and other dimensions, mandalas are often depicted in colored sands or paintings. They are mostly associated with Tibetan Buddhism.

The most famous Bodhisattva in existence today is the Dalai Lama. He is the reincarnation of Chenrezig, Bodhisattva of Compassion. The Dalai Lama is leader of Buddhism in Tibet, but also its political head of state. Exiled since the Chinese invasion of Tibet in 1949, he has become a beloved and respected ambassador for peace. A prolific author, charismatic lecturer, and extensive world traveler, his teachings of peace, compassion, and tolerance have reached the four corners of the globe, spreading a non-religious yet universal message.

Buddha

Siddhartha Gautauma, revered as Buddha ("the Awakened One"), was born to Hindu royal parents in Nepal in 566 BCE. His birth was preceded by omens predicting he would achieve Bodhi ("awakening") for the good of this world.

As a young man, he discovered the human suffering and death hidden from him all his life and became a wandering ascetic (Shramana). Close to death due to extreme fasting and self-denial, he saw this way as fruitless.

It was following the "middle way" between extremes of self-denial and self-indulgence that he found enlightenment about Dharma (truth) under the Bodhi tree and became a Buddha.

Traveling forty-five years throughout the Indian subcontinent, he taught the sutras (sermons) and achieved Nirvana at his death, ending his cycle of reincarnations.

Hinduism honors Buddha as the ninth incarnation of Lord Shiva, and many teachings have been incorporated in its dogma.

Spiritual Eye Prayer /
Paramahansa Yogananda

Paramahansa Yogananda

Born in India in 1893, Paramahansa Yogananda showed an early awareness and desire for the spiritual. Seeking guidance on his spiritual path to enlightenment, he became the disciple of Swami Sri Yukteswar Giri, a revered master of yoga and a monk in the Swami order.

He founded a school in India, where spiritual teachings and yoga were instructed along with modern academics, and gained a widespread reputation for his teachings and achievements in education.

He is the first master of yoga to have settled in the West in 1920 and to reveal the ancient teaching and practice of yoga. Through many books and acclaimed lectures in America and Europe, he introduced practical ways of meditation and how to apply them to everyday life to millions.

He led his life by his principle of finding happiness and inner peace through self-mastery and meditation. Preaching religious tolerance and goodwill, he advocated peace and the personal realization of the divine in each of us.

Yogananda died in 1952, achieving mahasamadhi, or "God-realized soul final exit from the body."

The Self-Realization Fellowship, founded in 1920, continues to educate, inspire and teach Kriya Yoga, the ancient Indian soul-awakening technique Yogananda revived and into which he initiated Mahatma Gandhi. SRF Meditation centers offer peaceful and beautiful surroundings, open to visitors and adepts.

Yoga

Yoga ("union") is an ancient complex Hindu practice with origins tracing back to the ancient sacred texts of Hinduism, dated several millennia ago. Part of the initiation into spiritual development, a privileged way of achieving union with the God inside oneself, it is taught by teachers (gurus).

In its original form, yoga is a deeply elaborate system of mental, physical, and psychological exercises, promoting self-awareness, with the goal of reaching control, increasing the life force, obtaining stillness of the mind, then spiritual insight. Living life without disturbing one's peace of mind is encouraged at all levels and times.

Adepts are instructed to follow five practices: proper poses (asanas), proper breathing (pranayama), proper relaxation (savasana), proper diet (vegetarianism) and meditation.

Asanas bring physical benefits and wellbeing to the practitioner. Pranayama, the technique of controlling one's breath, increases the life force and mental clarity.

Savasana promotes quietness and rejuvenation. Vegetarianism keeps the body free of animal karma and aligns with Ahimsa, the Hindu concept of non-violence. Meditation prepares and allows for spiritual insight and enlightenment.

Many different schools of thought have developed over the centuries, leading to different yoga poses, philosophies, and techniques. They include Ananda (which includes silent affirmations during asanas), Hatha (most widely used, it has thousands of poses), Ashtanga (moving from posture to posture without pause), Iyengar (poses are held longer, with focus on proper alignment), Bikram (done in a heated room), and Kriya (developed by Yogananda).

The influence of yoga into everyday life has grown tremendously since being introduced to the West a century ago. Meditation and the practice of yoga no longer are defined as religious or spiritual practices. They are used widely for stress reduction, physical wellbeing, mental focus, and emotional control, to name a few uses. Yoga brings enormous benefits to its adepts, many of whom are not aware of the deep spiritual meaning and power it carries.

The use of meditation as a tool toward enlightenment has been included and further extended in Buddhism, Jainism, and other philosophies. Islam and Christianity have taken stands to denounce yoga as an unhealthy practice.

"WE RETURN THANKS" /
IROQUOIS

Iroquois

The Iroquois tribe is based in upper New York State and Canada. Composed of six nations, its constitution is several centuries old.

The tribes trace their origin back to the holy being Sky Woman, who fell from the sky. She formed earth and her flora and gave birth to twins representing good and evil. The constant need for balance between these forces is at the root of Iroquois beliefs.

While the belief in Great Spirit is shared with other North American tribes, man's role and importance in the way of things are less significant, less important. Man is at the mercy of evil spirits, which can be frightened away with special dances, and the wearing of scary masks. Ceremonies are geared towards more concrete and less spiritual goals, such as physical healing or harvest.

Iroquois place a large import on dreams, believed to be the privileged way of communication with the soul. Many of the masks used in healing ceremonies are the result of a dreamed vision.

The Iroquois resisted the coming of Christianity and held onto their rituals until tribe member Handsome Lake had visions in 1799. Teaching the blending of traditional religion and rites alongside Christian concepts, he founded the Longhouse religion, still practiced today.

SERENITY PRAYER /
REINHOLD NIEBUHR

Reinhold Niebuhr (1892–1971)

Reinhold Niebuhr was born in Missouri, of German ancestry. He became a minister in the German Evangelical Synod, a denomination emphasizing daily spiritual practice over dogma.

Often at odds with other Christians, he believed that today's injustice could not be ignored for the promise and hope of future redemption, the daily practical demonstration of one's spirituality being more important than theological discourses.

A minister in Detroit, he became aware of and outraged at the difficult lives of American factory workers, especially in the auto industry. He fought their apathy, which he blamed on the misplaced idealism and unrealistic teachings of the mainstream Christian doctrine. Part religious leader, part social advocate, he supported a socialist-style economy, based on the human treatment and the moral consideration of workers before personal gain.

Leaving pastoral work to turn to a socio-political career, he wrote and lectured on social and economic justice for all. He opposed the government infringement on civil liberties in the name of national security during WWII, even though he was a strong supporter of U.S. involvement in the war.

A journalist, lobbyist, and teacher, his work still resonates today.

This prayer is famous as part of Alcoholic Anonymous and other Twelve Step programs. It was written in the 1930s.

THE GREAT INVOCATION/ MAITREYA

Maitreya

Lord Maitreya is known as the Buddha of future age, the next Bodhisattva to enter the world. He embodies compassion and teaches humanity the pure dharma. He is the successor of Gautama Buddha.

This prayer is not Buddhist in origin and refers to Maitreya as the awaited world teacher.

Alice Bailey is credited with channeling this prayer in 1937. Influenced by theosophy, her vast and complex esoteric teachings describe an elaborate spiritual hierarchy, of which Maitreya is the Ascended Master who will emerge to lead the planet to a New and Golden Age.

For some New Age movements, Maitreya is to be the tenth and final incarnation of Hindu Vishnu, Kalki Avatar, the Christian Christ, the Jewish Messiah, and Islam's Imam Mahdi. A world teacher embracing all religions as a path to God, he is seen as the universal One who will return to unify all people and religions, and bring universal peace.

Prayer to Practice the Golden Rule/ Eusebius of Caesarea

Eusebius of Caesarea

Little is known of the early life of Eusebius.

Bishop of Caesarea in Palestine in the fourth century CE, Eusebius is known for his prolific writings.

He was a scholar and ecclesiastical historian who wrote treatises on doctrinal matters, biographies of martyrs, and the history of the church. Said to be a historian as well as a history maker, his writings remain controversial to this day. He is called the "father of church history" for his recording of the history of early Christianity.

Please refer to "Christianity" and "Jesus Christ" sections under "Peace Prayer/St. Francis."

LIGHT INVOCATION/ DAEL WALKER

DaEl Walker

DaEl Walker wrote this incantation in 1980, originally as a personal tool of protection, which he shares with all.

DaEl Walker is a world-renowned expert on the healing powers of crystals. As founder and director of the Crystal Awareness Institute, he has been lecturing and teaching for twenty-five years. His books on the subject are authoritative, and his research extensive. His study of alternative energy therapies includes crystal, color, touch and prayer.

DaEl walker has also worked extensively with crystal skulls, including the famed Mitchell-Hedges Skull. He is the guardian of the Rainbow Skull.

These skulls, thirteen in total and made of clear or colored crystal, have been found in Mexico, in Central and South America. Of unknown origin, age, and manufacture, the mystery that surrounds them, has led to numerous hypotheses as to their source, as varied as from extraterrestrials, lost Atlantis, pre-Columbian, or nineteenth century fakes. As with other artifacts of unexplained origin, they are said to have magical healing powers. They might change color, emit sounds, and affect people handling them in different physiological ways.

Presence of the Divine Light / Sri Swami Satchidananda

Sri Swami Satchidananda

His Holiness Sri Swami Satchidananda was an influential and beloved yoga master. Born in India in 1914, he started his spiritual journey after the death of his beloved wife. He would study under several great spiritual masters and became a follower of Swami Sivananda.

While living at an ashram in Sri Lanka, he taught yoga and worked on modernizing the ancient rules and practices of the community to adapt to a changing world.

In 1966, he moved to the U.S., spreading his message of harmony among all faiths and races. Gaining attention as the opening speaker at the Woodstock festival, Sri Swami Satchidananda extended his teachings by authoring books and giving countless lectures. The founder of Integral Yoga® and of the ashram Yogaville in Virginia, his mission has touched and inspired people of all ways of life. He died in 2002.

His message highlights the universal truth at the core of many world religions. He believes that individual transformation can lead to world unity and harmony, urges us on to stop hurting each other, and encourages us to serve each other instead. One finds happiness inside oneself, with positive thinking leading the self-change that starts within then extends outward. Peace of mind cannot be brought in; it originates and develops from inside.

Integral yoga helps achieve balance of one's body, mind, and emotions. A combination of various other branches of yoga, its role is to calm the mind and bring harmony to the adept.

Please refer to "Yoga" section under "Spiritual Eye Prayer/ Yagananda Paramahansa."

Prayer for Peace / Zoroastrianism

Zoroastrianism

The oldest revealed monotheistic religion, Zoroastrianism is believed to have appeared at around 1,000 to 1,500 BCE.

In Ancient Persia (present day Iran), the Prophet Zoroaster (also called Zarathustra) introduced the worship of the one God Ahuma Mazda (Wise Lord). Anghra Mainuy, creator of destruction, represents evil. This cosmic battle takes place in humans and will ultimately result in the victory of the forces of good. At that time of last judgment, a savior (Saoshyant) will appear.

Zathushtra compiled the Gathas, seventeen divine revelations in hymns and poems. Handed down orally for generations, they were finally written down into the Avesta, along with more contemporary texts and commentaries named Pahlavi. Expressing ideas of compassion and universal order, these ideas were later taught by Greek philosophers, and influenced Judaism, Christianity, Islam, and Northern India Buddhism.

Zoroastrianism is based on the doctrine of "Asha," meaning truth, righteousness. Man is uniquely responsible for the fate of his soul and that of the world, and cannot count on divine intervention. One's salvation depends on his free will, his acceptance of personal responsibility, and on the practice of daily cleansing and prayer rituals. The threefold path, "good thoughts, good words, good deeds," is the motto of the followers. Fire symbolizing the original light of God holds a sacred place in rituals and festivals.

The collective celebrations of seven annual feasts created a community united by beliefs and shared moral tenets. A new society emerged in this fertile region of Persia, bringing unity, prosperity, and political power that spread and helped sustain one of the great world empires for centuries.

Zoroastrianism is still practiced today, mostly in Iran and India.

"DISTURB US, LORD" / SIR FRANCIS DRAKE

Sir Francis Drake

Born in 1545, Sir Francis Drake is famous for his naval achievements.

The first Englishman to circumnavigate the world, he was commissioned by Queen Elizabeth I. His first voyage, as opposed to Magellan's, would take him from the Atlantic to the Pacific Ocean via South America. It would last three years and involve sea and land exploration and the claiming of new lands, as well as the plundering of enemy Spanish ships and colonies for riches and spices. Other voyages led to increasing battles with the Spanish navy, culminating in the attempted invasion of England by Spain in 1588. Vice Admiral Drake's naval strategy led to the routing of the Spanish Armada. This victory propelled England as a dominant world powerhouse, and he would come to be known as "the pioneer of the British Empire."

A man of action, not ideas, he used piracy, the trade of slaves, and greedy dishonesty to amass a fortune. Knighted by Elizabeth I, he was given the title of "privateer" allowing him to claim (stolen) goods in the Queen's name. His aggressive attacks against and plundering of Catholic

Spanish and Portuguese ships led to the decline of their dominance of the trade routes.

He is credited with having written this prayer as he departed Portsmouth to raid Spanish strongholds in South America, during which trip he died of fever.

Please refer to "Christianity" and "Jesus Christ" sections under "Peace Prayer/St. Francis."

LOTUS SUTRA/ NICHIREN BUDDHISM

Lotus Sutra

The meaning and power of the Lotus Sutra (Odaimoku = Sacred Title) were revealed to Nichiren Shonin, a Japanese Buddhist priest, on April 28, 1253.

Containing all the benefits of Buddha's wisdom, its chanting gives everyone on earth the potential to obtain and establish an enlightened way of life. It is the expression in words of Buddha's Law of Life and eternal truths.

Containing twenty-eight chapters, it translates as "Adoration to the Scripture of the Lotus of the Perfect Truth."

Nichiren Shonin

Born in a fisherman family in thirteenth-century Japan, Nichiren Shonin became a Buddhist priest. He studied intensively for twenty years before concluding that the Lotus Sutra condensed the perfect teaching of the Buddha.

Preaching its message of accessibility to Buddhahood through the sutra, he urged people to stop the practice of superstitions and other misguided beliefs, and turn toward the happiness and enlightenment contained in it. The sutra gave Buddha's qualities and wisdom to the individual, regardless of life circumstances. It offered all the potential of the highest success.

The violent negative reaction of the authorities to his treatises on governmental shortcomings and established religion's mistaken teachings forced him into exile. He was able to complete more writings before his death in 1282.

The Buddhist school he founded, Nichiren Shu, is still active today and growing around the world. Adepts perform five practices around the Lotus Sutra: receiving and keeping it in the body and mind, reading it with the eyes, reciting it, explaining it to others, and copying it.

Its message of universal access to the state of Buddhahood through the sutra has spread throughout the globe.

Please refer to "Buddha" and "Buddhism" section under "Mantra of Compassion" and "Om."

FIRE BLESSING /
ABORIGINE

Aborigine

The aborigine term refers to the indigenous inhabitants of Australia and the surrounding islands and to their culture.

Several hundred independent nations with their own languages are united in their strong spirituality and painful colonial experience.

In the aborigine creation myth, the first beings came forth out of Dreamtime. Dreamtime represents the Great Spirit Ancestor, the beginning of knowledge and of the laws of human existence. From darkness emerged Ancestral Beings, who created the land, bodies of water, people, animals and plants, the three elements (air, water, and fire) as well as the planets. Returning to a state of sleep, they merged their spirits into sacred life forms or places such as Ayers Rock.

Man remains an integral part of the world, with close ties and equal footing with nature. All parts of the natural world have a spirit, to be honored and revered.

Aborigines today continue this vibrant tradition through ceremonies, music, and dances, which recall the power of creation. Traditions and stories that have been transmitted orally for generations and over tens of thousands of years are kept alive through secret rites and initiations.

Paintings of the body, rocks, and wood carry the designs of the unbroken relationship with the Ancestral Beings and the deep connection with the land. A bamboo flute, of about five feet, is used for formal ceremonies and is called a didgeridoo.

The colonization of Australia in the late nineteenth century led to massive negative changes for this population. Land expropriation, the introduction of new diseases, the forced exile to urban areas, and widespread poverty led to decades of abuse and marginalization. In the last thirty years, the restoration of property and rights has become at the front of Australian political life.

PRAYER OF PROSPERITY / ZEN BUDDHISM

Zen

A school of Buddhism mostly prevalent in Japan, Zen teaches that the potential to reach enlightenment is present in all men.

Zen, which traces back to China in the sixth century CE, refuses established religious practices. Zen rejects rituals, theoretical information, personal codes of ethics and ways of worship.

Sitting or walking meditation is the privileged tool to go beyond words in order to achieve understanding of the meaning of life. Breath control helps the adept stay focused in the present. Intuitive understanding is the key to the state of being where logic is irrelevant and words only have meaning for the one who is using them.

Adepts meditate on koans, riddles without an obvious solution, sometimes for years. Mental thought patterns must be released during meditation so that the koan's true meaning is revealed. The koan, "Two hands clap, and there is a sound. What is the sound of one hand clapping?" is well known.

The quiet contemplation of beautiful and tranquil gardens is part of the meditative practice. Zen has come to reflect peace, tranquility, sobriety of forms and thoughts, and meditative silence. Its influence on the Japanese culture has been extensive, as reflected in the custom of such traditions as flower arrangement or the tea ceremony,

Mahaprajna-paramita, the "heart of the perfection of great wisdom" mantra, has been invoked by all Buddhas to obtain complete and perfect enlightenment.

Zen Buddhism is widely practiced around the globe.

Please refer to "Buddha" and "Buddhism" section under "Mantra of Compassion" and "Om."

Peace Prayer/Kikuyu

Kikuyu

The largest ethnic group in Kenya, eastern Africa, the Kikuyu have a long religious tradition.

Chosen by Ngai, the Supreme Being, a Bantu man named Gikuyu was led to sacred Mount Kirinyaga (today known as Mt. Kenya) to become the father of a new tribe. From his nine daughters were established nine clans.

African religions are as colorful and diverse as the languages, culture, and practices of each small familial or communal group where they originated in.

With no written set of rules and no specific religious leader, religion is part of life, and rites of passage become expressions of belief. Prayers, music, dance, and sacrifice are rituals supervised by elders, shared by the community, and usually carried out under a sacred tree or mountain.

Handed down through time, stories, myths, proverbs, and legends stress the lack of distinction between the sacred and the mundane. Shamans communicate with gods and guardian spirits for guidance and help.

Colonization brought the main religions to Africa, and many communities have blended traditions and rituals. Today, most Kikuyu are Christians.

Farming and the husbandry of domesticated animals are predominant to this day. Kikuyu also are political, educational, and cultural leaders.

MUHAMMAD'S PRAYER / ISLAM

Muhammed

Muhammed ibn Abdallah was born in modern Saudi Arabia in 570 CE and died in 632 CE. A man of exceptional character and honesty, he received Allah's messages through the archangel Gabriel, prophesying for thirteen years.

He based Islam's doctrine on the strict adherence to the five pillars (see below), and transmitted revelations as well as a way of life. His life is an example of the qualities that shape Islam: sanctity, wisdom, generosity, justice, humanity, modesty, and integrity.

His teachings spread rapidly among the Arabian tribes, and Islamic rule was applied to the communities' political, legal, and religious life.

Islam

The last monotheistic religion, Islam emerged in the sixth century in the Arabian Peninsula.

Received by Muhammed the Prophet, Allah's revelations are compiled in the Koran (Qur'an). The Hadith is the collection of the record of Muhammad's life and sayings. The code of regulations that emerged from their interpretation is called the Sharia.

Islam shares the Old Testament, prophets, and holy sites with Judaism and Christianity. While doctrine distinctions appeared due to the vast range of ethnic, national, and cultural differences in the Muslim world, the Sharia is at the base of Muslim life and defines the ideal order for every human activity. Islam requires the believer to submit in body and mind to the will of Allah (One God), and so to bring order and harmony to the world (Salam or Peace). Every Muslim's responsibility is to lead a pious, charitable, life and study the Koran (Tawhid).

Muslims believe that Allah and his prophets, angels, and messengers bring guidance to men (Nubuwwa), and that divine judgment is based on one's life (Maad).

The believer follows the five pillars: Shaha dah (witnessing that there is no God worthy of worship except Allah and that Muhammed is his messenger), Salah (ritual prayer of worship five times a day), fasting during the month of Ramadan, Zakat (charity), and Hajj (once a lifetime pilgrimage to Mecca).

Physical purity and ritual cleansing (Salat) as well as specific postures and directions are most important during prayers.

Islam is present in everyday life from education or artistic recitations to governmental laws. Though several branches of Islam disagree on the Sharia, Islam has flourished throughout the ages and around the world, creating administrative and legal models, making essential scientific discoveries, and mastering mathematics, astronomy, art, calligraphy, and architecture.

Today's Muslims however are seeing escalating conflicts between opposed sects and division regarding the strictness of adherence to the Sharia in a changing world. The two major groups in opposition today are Sunnis and Shiites. Sunni Muslims strictly follow Muhammad's teachings and examples, or "sunnah," believing them to be the pillars of the faith. Shiite Muslims believe that Muhammad's descendants through Ali, his cousin and son-in-law, are his legitimate successors. Called imams, they are venerated as direct intermediaries with God, their words believed to be divinely inspired. Though Shiites constitute a minority in the Muslim world, the extremist views and bloody following of some imams by various factions have created political and philosophical conflict within the Islamic faith and beyond.

SPIRIT /'ABDU'L-BAHA

'Abdu'l-Baha

The son and successor of the second prophet Baha'u'llah, he is considered one of the prophets of Ba'hai. Born in 1844, he studied extensively the writings of Bab, as well as verses from the Qur'an before becoming the head of the movement founded by his father. A prolific writer, his views a century ago remain contemporary today.

Traveling throughout the world, he proclaimed and spread Baha'i. Widely known as an ambassador of world peace, he embodies the spirit of unity, justice, and harmony of his faith.

Baha'i

This young monotheistic religious movement preaches that God continually offers humanity guidance through prophets ("Manifestations of God"), regardless of religion and time, as well as in the sacred writings of various creeds. Unity, equality, and universal peace are at the core of its teachings.

Revelations are given via inspirations, contemplation, and scientific advances. They are updated and adapted to suit a particular time and place, while older traditions are abandoned when no longer suitable.

Baha'I emphasizes consistent principles: love of God, moral purity, fraternity, fasting, service, justice, detachment of material concerns, and education.

Founded in Persia in 1863 by Baha'u'llah, the Baha'i faith is based on the divine revelations to the three central figures: the Bab ("Gate" and precursor of the movement), Baha'u'llah ("Glory of God" and his follower), and 'Abdu'l-Baha ("Servant of Baha," and Baha'u'llah's son).

Preaching the belief that every religion worships the same God under a different name, the Baha'i faith is expanding through the globe. This peaceful movement has gained adepts as the new unifying religion. Incorporating teachings of all faiths, the Baha'i vision is of the oneness of global society, with justice, peace, harmony, equality, and prosperity for all people.

Its followers are persecuted in Islamic countries, which see them as having rejected their original Islamic Shiite faith.

PROTECTION PRAYER / ISABEL HICKEY

Isabel Hickey

Known as Issie, Isabel Hickey (1903–1980) followed in the footsteps of Evangeline Adams, known as the mother of spiritual astrology.

Her teachings and work revolutionized astrology in the '60s and '70s. Her books introduced a more accessible, valuable, and positive astrology, a worthwhile tool on one's spiritual journey.

With her interpretation, a horoscope loses its dark, fatalistic quality, becoming a positive and helpful instrument of guidance. No longer unalterable, one's chart becomes fluid and ever changing. It offers information about planetary influences, helping with making sound decisions, or taking advantage of opportunities. The chart reveals one's strengths and weaknesses favorable or unsuitable time periods, as well as areas of needed spiritual and karmic work.

GLOSSARY

Adam and Eve: first humans whose disobedience of God's rule lead to their expulsion from the Garden of Eden. For Christians, this constitutes the original sin.

Ahimsa: principle of non-violence.

Angel: heavenly being, messenger of God.

Archangel: angel of a higher rank.

Armada: Spanish Navy, defeated by the English in 1588.

Asana: yoga pose.

Ascended Master: self-realized being who chooses to remain on the earth plane to help humanity.

Ascetic: discipline or philosophy based on austerity and self-denial.

Ashram: of Hindu origin, a place of instruction usually of a spiritual nature.

Astrology: study of planetary positions and their influence.

Avatar: incarnation, usually of a Hindu god, onto human form.

Avesta: sacred book of Zoroastrianism.

Ayers Rock: "Uluru," sacred aborigine mountain in Australia.

Bantu: largest tribe of Eastern and Southern Africa.

Baptism: ritual of acceptance into the Christian religion, sprinkling of holy water or immersion into water.

Bhagavat Gita: most sacred Hindu epic poem, collection of Krishna's teachings.

Bible: Holy book for Jews (Old Testament) and Christians (Old and New Testaments).

Bodhi: Buddhist state of enlightenment.

Bodhisattva: he/she who has attained Nirvana, but has delayed entrance to remain on the earth plane and help humanity.

Brahman: Hindu Godhead, and the Divine in all living things.

Brahmin: Hindu priest.

Buddha: "Enlightened One, name given to those who have achieved Nirvana; name given to Siddharta Gautama, founder of Buddhism".

Channeling: receiving messages from other planes of existence while in trance or meditative state.

Chart: astrological diagram showing the position of planets at one's birth (horoscope).

Covenant: sacred agreement.

Crucifixion: ancient form of execution, involving the nailing of the condemned to an upright cross until death.

Dharma: Buddhist and Hindu laws of conduct, doctrine, righteous duty.

Dhikr: for Muslims remembrance of name of God; recitation of the names of God for Sufis.

Diaspora: exile of the Jewish community.

Dogma: set of religious beliefs held true by its followers.

Dreamtime: aborigine creation myth.

Eight-Fold Path: Buddhist ways to attain Nirvana: right view, thought, action, speech, effort, remembrance, livelihood, and concentration.

Elements: fire, water and earth, with wood, air or metal in some philosophies.

Esoteric: secret, revealed only to initiates.

Fasting: practice of voluntarily abstaining from food.

Five Pillars of Islam: daily confession of faith (shahada), daily prayers (Salat), mandatory donation (zakat), fasting during Ramadan (sawm), and pilgrimage to Mecca (Hajj).

Four-Fold Benefaction: Sources to whom one owes one's life: heaven and earth, parents, brethren, and religious laws.

Garden of Eden: place where Adam and Eve lived.

Gathas: Zoroaster's seventeen songs.

Gayatri: Goddess-mother, the feminine aspect of Brahman.

Godhead: nature, essence of the Divine/God.

Gospel: teachings of Jesus Christ.

Great Spirit: Godhead for American Indian tribes.

Guru: spiritual or religious leader and teacher.

Hadith: collection of Muhammad's sayings.

Hajj: Pilgrimage to Mecca.

Heaven: for Christians, where God dwells, the goal and reward of human existence.

Hell: for Christians, where the devil dwells and damned souls go after death.

Hermit: person rejecting social interaction as a spiritual or religious practice.

Holy Spirit: Third part of the Trinity for Christians, name given to earthly signs of the presence of God for Jews.

Incantation: ritual chant, often thought magical.

Islam: the religion of Muslims, means "surrender."

Jerusalem: holy city of Judaism, Muslims, and Christians, in present-day Israel.

Karma: "action"; cosmic law of cause and effect.

Koan: Zen Buddhist riddle.

Koran: holy book of Islam.

Kosher: Jewish dietary laws.

Magellan: sixteenth century Portuguese explorer, first to circle the globe.

Mahaprajna Paramita: "the Heart Sutra," one of greatest mantras.

Mahayana: Buddhist philosophy including Zen, Tibetan, Vijnanavada schools.

Mahasattva: a Bodhisattva who has achieved enlightenment.

Mandala: "circle"; cosmic representation.

Mantra: "hymn," word or sound whose repetition leads to spiritual awakening.

Martyr: person who sacrifices himself for his religious beliefs.

Mecca: birthplace of Muhammad, in present Saudi Arabia.

Meditation: technique using the emptying of one's mind, directed concentration in order to achieve relaxation or contemplation.

Messiah: for Christians Jesus Christ; for Jews the anointed king who will lead them back to Israel.

Moksha: release from cycle of reincarnation in Hinduism.

Monotheism: religious belief in one God.

New Age: recent movement rejecting established dogma in favor of seeking Universal Truth and the highest human potential through spiritual practices drawn from all religions and philosophies, and including astrology, cosmic laws, ecology, naturopathy, and other esoteric teachings.

New Testament: second part of the Christian Bible, relating to Jesus Christ's life and teachings.

Ngai: Supreme God of the Kikuyu tribe.

Nirvana: for Buddhism, goal of human life, the end of cycle of birth and rebirth, enlightenment and the cessation of pain.

Odaimoku: sacred title of the "lotus sutra."

Old Testament: first part of the Bible, relating the creation of the world and the history of ancient Hebrews.

Paramita: stage of spiritual perfection, achieved by boddhisattvas.

Persia: ancient empire in present Iraq, Iran, and Syria.

Pranayama: breath control technique.

Prophet: transmitter and translator of divine will and rules.

Ramadan: ninth month of the Islamic calendar, during which fasting is required from dawn to sundown.

Repentance: regret, contrition.

Resurrection: rising of the dead in Christian belief.

Sacrifice: the giving of a valued object, or self, to a god as a form of worship.

Salah (or Salat): mandatory prayers for Muslims, performed five times a day.

Samsara: the opposition of Nirvana, cycle of reincarnation.

Self-Realization: complete union with God.

Seven Ceremonies: sacred Lakota Sioux rites.

Shaman: medium between humanity and the spirit world, by means of spiritual or magical rituals.

Sharia: Islam's holy law.

Shia: branch of Islam considering Ali, Muhammad's cousin and son-in-law and his descendants the imams, as true successors.

Shramana: ascetic wandering monk in the Hindu and Buddhist traditions.

Sky Woman: goddess of Iroquois creation myth.

Sunnism: branch of Islam, based on the Koran, Hadith, and Sharia, rather than devotion to the imams.

Sutra: brief summary of the teachings of Hinduism; also short text based on the words of Buddha.

Swami: Hindu religious teacher.

Talmud: compilation of writings forming Jewish Laws, consisting of the Mishnah and Gemura.

Tanach: sacred book of Judaism, Bible.

Tawhid: "unity," of God and of each Muslim with God.

Ten Commandments: given by God to Moses, they are at the core of Judeo-Christianity.

Theosophy: movement founded in the nineteenth century, based on complex cosmic, scientific, and metaphysical concepts, and the acceptance that Truth exists in all religions and philosophies.

Theravada: oldest and most traditional school of Buddhism.

Three Evil Paths: in Buddhism, the lowest realms (hell, hungry ghost, and animal).

Torah: for Judaism, first five books of the Bible.

Trimutri: the Hindu Trinity representing the three aspects of God.

Triple World: "universe" in Buddhism, it is comprised of the world of desires, the world of bodily form, and the immaterial world.

Twelve-Step Program: program helping people recover from behavior of abuse and addictions.

Vedas: holy scriptures of the Brahman/Hindu religion.

Vegetarianism: dietary law of non-violence directed by Hinduism and Buddhism and prohibiting the eating of any animal flesh.

Yoga: discipline born in India, "union with God" through physical postures.

Zakat: mandatory charitable donation for Muslims.

Zen: school of Japanese Buddhism.

Zionism: political movement to establish the Jewish state of Israel.

BIBLIOGRAPHY

Armstrong, Karen, *A history of God*. New York NY: Ballantine Books, 1993.

Bentounes, Khaled, *Sufism: the heart of Islam*. Prescott AZ: Hohm Press, 2002.

Boyce, Mary, *Zoroastrians: their religious beliefs and practices*. Routledge & Kegan Paul, 1984.

Burns, Paul, *Butler's lives of the saints*. Collegeville, Minn.: Liturgical Press, 2003.

Cleary, Thomas, transl., *Living and dying with grace: counsels of Hadrat' Ali*. Boston MA: Shambala Publications, 1995.

Crème, Benjamin, *Maitreya's mission*. Amsterdam, Los Angeles CA: Share International Foundation, 1993.

_____, *The Ageless Wisdom Teaching*. London: Share International Foundation, 2006

Davis Oliver, edit, *Celtic spirituality*. New York NY: Paulist Press 1999.

De Waal, Esther, *The Celtic way of prayer*. New York NY: Doubleday, 1997.

Devi, Nischala Joy, *The secret power of yoga*. New York NY: Three Rivers Press, 2007.

di Nola, Alfonas, *The prayers of man*. New York, NY: Obolensky Inc., 1961.

Earhart H. Byron, edit, *Religious traditions of the world*. New York NY: HarperCollins, 1993.

Eckel Malcolm David, *Buddhism*: origins, beliefs, practices, holy texts, sacred places. Oxford: Oxford University Press, 1946.

Ernst, Carl W. Ph.D., transl., *Teachings of Hadrat Ali*. Boston MA: Shambala Press, 1999.

Feuerstein, Georg & Bodian, Stephan, *Living Yoga: a comprehensive guide for daily life*. New York NY: J.P.Tarcher/Persee, 1993.

Feuerstein, Georg, *Shambala encyclopedia of yoga*. Boston MA: Shambala Publications Inc, 1997.

Fitzgerald, Judith & Oren Fitzgerald, Michael, editors,*The universal spirit of Islam from the Koran and the Hadith*. Bloomington IN: Word Wisdom, 2006.

Goddard, Dwight, compiled by, *The Lankavatra sutra: an epitomized version*. Rhineback NY: Monkfish Book publishing, 2003.

Gordon, Matthew S., *Islam*: origins, practices, holy texts, sacred persons, sacred places. Oxford: Oxford University Press, 2002.

Hartz, Paula, *Zoroastrianism*. New York NY: Facts on File, 1999.

_____, *Native American religions*. New York NY: Facts on File, 1997.

Hassaballa Hesham A. & Helminski, Kabir, *Islam*. Doubleday. c2006

Hassin, Vijay, *Modern Yoga Handbook*. Garden City NY: Dolphin books, 1978.

Huyler, Stephen P,*Meeting God: elements of Hindu devotion*. Newhaven and London: Yale university Press, 1999.

Hyde Paine, Mabel, compiled by,*The divine art of living*. Wilmette IL: Baha'I Publishing, 2006.

Kahn, Hazrat Inayat, *The mysticism of sound and music*. Boston MA: Shambala publications, 1996.

Kelsey, Harry, *Sir Francis Drake: the Queen's pirate*. New Haven: Yale University Press, 1998.

Lugina, Aloysius M, *African religion*. New York, NY: Facts on File, 1999.

Mandel Kahn, Gabriel, *Buddha*. San Diego CA: Thunder Bay Press, 2004.

Matthews, Caitlin & John, *Encyclopedia of Celtic wisdom: the Celtic shaman's sourcebook*. Shaftsbury Dorset, Rockport MA: Element Books, 1994.

Merriam-Webster's, *Encyclopedia of world religions*. Merriam-Webster Inc., 1999.

Myss, Caroline. *Entering the Castle: an inner path to God and your soul*. New York NY: Free Press, 2007.

Rabey, Steve, *in the house of memory*. New York NY: Dutton 1998.

Sardar, Ziauddin & Abbas Malik, Zafar, *Introducing Muhammad*. Cambridge: Icon books, 1999.

Schmidt, Jeff, *365 Buddha: daily meditations*. New York NY: Jeremy P. Tarcher, 2002.

Sifton, Elisabeth, *The serenity prayer*. London, England: W.W. Norton & Co Ltd, 2003.

Smith, Peter. *The Baha'i religion*. Oxford, England: George Ronald, 1996.

Stone, Joshua David Ph.D., *Hidden mysteries*. Sedona AZ: Light Technology Publishing, 1995.

_____, *A beginner's guide to ascension*. Sedona AZ: Light Technology Publishing, 1998.

Swami Aiswarananda, *Meditation and its practices: a definite guide to techniques and traditions of meditation in yoga and vedanta*. Woodstock VT: Skylight Paths Publishing, 2003.

Wilson, Mike, *World religion*. Detroit: Greenhaven Press, 2006.

Whitfield, Peter, *Sir Francis Drake*. New York NY: New York University Press, 2004.

Yogananda, Paramahansa, *Autobiography of a yogi*. Self-Realization Fellowship, 1946.

_____, *To be victorious in life*. Self-Realization Fellowship, 2002.

Websites

people.bu.edu
www.aboriginalaustralia.com
www.africaguide.com
www.allaboutprayer.org
www.allabouttruth.org
www.archaeology.org
www.ascendedmasters.com
www.avesta.org
www.bahai.org
www.blessingscornucopia.com
www.britannia.com
www.buddhadharma.org
www.buddhistdoor.com
www.ccel.org
www.christianitytoday.com
www.crystalawareness.com
www.crystalinks.com
www.cs.williams.edu
www.dalailama.com
www.dharma-haven.org
www.dharmaweb.org
www.elexion.com/lakota
www.enchantedlearning.com/explorers
www.everyculture.com
www.gayatrimantra.net
geneva.rutgers.edu
www.godprayers.org

www.greatdreams.com
www.greatsite.com
www.great-spirit-mother.org
www.hinduismtoday.com
www.indianetzone.com
www.indigenouspeople.net
www.interfacecentre.org.au
www.iroquois.net
www.islamawareness.net
www.islamreligion.com
www.jannah.org
www.jewishvirtuallibrary.org
www.kenya-information-guide.com
www.maitreya.org
www.nichiren-shu.org
www.nichirenshoshumyoshinji.org
www.om-guru.com
www.religionfacts.com
www.sacred-texts.com
www.sgi-usa.org
www.solsticepoint.com
www.sufimovement.org
www.swamisatchidananda.org
www.uga.edu
www.urbandharma.org
www.world-mysteries.com
www.yogaville.org
www.zarathushtra.com
zen.rinnou.net
www.12step.org

Photographs

The Peace Prayer/St. Francis
Oowenoc
Dreamstime.com

Gayatri Mantra
dharma-haven.org

Prayer for Peace/Khan
Flockholl
Dreamstime.com

O Great Spirit
Mygdalaim
Dreamstime.com

Guidance Prayer
Erickn
Dreamstime.com

Mantra of Compassion
Michael Barber
123rf.com

Spiritual Eye Prayer
Sybille Yates
123rf.com

We return Thanks Prayer
Dieonis
Dreamtime.com

The Healing Prayer
Hypermania 2
123rf.com

Serenity Prayer
Author's private collection: Hawaiian Skies

The Great Invocation
ELEN Art
123rf.com

Om
Kailash Soni
123.rf.com

Golden Rule Prayer
Anp
123.rf

Light Invocation
Alex Lapuerta Mediavilla
123.rf.com

Presence of the Divine Light
ELEN Art
123.rf.com

Prayer for Peace/Zoroastrian
PaulPaladin
123rf.com

Disturb us Lord
Ironrodart
Dreamstime.com

Lotus Sutra
Dragonjian
Dreamstime.com

Strength and Wisdom Prayer
ELEN Art
123.rf.com

Prayer of Prosperity
Michael Klenetsky
123rf.com

Peace Prayer/Kikuyu
Shevs
Dreamstime.com

Muhammad's Prayer
123.rf.com: Javarman Javarman

Spirit
Anp
123rf.com

Protection Prayer
Yang MingQi
123.rf.com

Made in the USA
Charleston, SC
02 August 2010